BETWEEN L[
Poems 1972–198[

BETWEEN LEAPS
Poems 1972–1985

Brad Leithauser

OXFORD UNIVERSITY PRESS
1987

Oxford University Press, Walton Street, Oxford OX2 6DP
Oxford   New York   Toronto
Delhi   Bombay   Calcutta   Madras   Karachi
Petaling Jaya   Singapore   Hong Kong   Tokyo
Nairobi   Dar es Salaam   Cape Town
Melbourne   Auckland
and associated companies in
Beirut   Berlin   Ibadan   Nicosia

Oxford is a trade mark of Oxford University Press
© Brad Leithauser 1987

The poems in this selection first published in Hundreds of Fireflies
(Knopf Poetry Series 6) 1982 and Cats of the Temple
(Knopf Poetry Series 20) 1986, both published by Alfred A. Knopf,
New York, USA
This selection first published as an Oxford University Press paperback 1987

All rights reserved. No part of this publication may be reproduced,
stored in a retrieval system, or transmitted, in any form or by any means,
electronic, mechanical, photocopying, recording, or otherwise, without
the prior permission of Oxford University Press

This book is sold subject to the condition that it shall not, by way
of trade or otherwise, be lent, re-sold, hired out or otherwise circulated
without the publisher's prior consent in any form of binding or cover
other than that in which it is published and without a similar condition
including this condition being imposed on the subsequent purchaser

British Library Cataloguing in Publication Data
Leithauser, Brad
Between leaps.
I. Title.
811'.54   PS3562.E4623
ISBN 0–19–282089–3

Set by Rowland Phototypesetting Ltd.
Printed in Great Britain by
J. W. Arrowsmith Ltd., Bristol

To Anthony Hecht

The words, although not mine,
Are both the next best thing and better yet:
They're yours. I'd borrow a line
Or two—perhaps, 'man hopes to learn
The leafy secret, pay his most outstanding debt'?—
To speak of obligations in my turn.

CONTENTS

The Ghost of a Ghost	3
Angel	6
Miniature	7
11 Astronomical Riddles	8
Odd Carnivores	10
Minims	11
Daybreak	12
Old Hat	13
A Rock with a View	14
A Michigan Ghost Town	16
Between Leaps	17
Duckweed	18
Along Lake Michigan	19
Birches	21
Additional Bats	22
A Quilled Quilt, A Needle Bed	23
Canoeing at Night	24
An Expanded Want Ad	26
Hundreds of Fireflies	29
The Return to a Cabin	31
Two Summer Jobs	33

* * *

Two Suspensions against a Blacktop Backdrop	41
The Buried Graves	43
An Actor Plays a Trumpet	44
Dainties: A Suite	46
A Stuffed Tortoise	50
Minims	51
Seahorses	53
A Noisy Sleeper	56
Floating Light in Tokyo	59
Hesitancy	61

In Minako Wada's House	63
The Tigers of Nanzen-Ji	65
In a Japanese Moss Garden	67
A Flight from Osaka	70
Seaside Greetings	71
On a Seaside Mountain	74
Two Incidents On and Off Guam	77

BETWEEN LEAPS

THE GHOST OF A GHOST

I

The pleasures I took from life
were simple things—to play catch
in the evenings with my son,
or tease my daughter (whom I addressed
as Princess Pea), or to watch
television, curled on the floor.
Sometimes I liked to drink too much,
but not too often. Perhaps best
of all was the delight I found
waking to a drowse at one
or two at night and my wife
huffing (soft, not quite a snore)
beside me, a comforting sound.

We had our problems of course,
Emily and I, occasions when
things got out of hand.—Once she threw
a juice glass at me that broke
on the wall (that night I drew
a face there, a clownish man
catching it square on the nose,
and Emily laughed till she cried).
It's true I threatened divorce
a few times (she did too), but those
were ploys, harmless because love ran
through every word we spoke—
and then, an accident, I died.

II

Afterwards, my kids began
having nightmares—when they slept
at all; Emily moved in a haze,
looking older, ruined now, and wept
often and without warning.

The rooms had changed, become mere
photographs in which my face
was oddly missing . . . That first year
without me: summer twilight, and those
long leaf-raking Saturdays
without me, and Christmas morning—
the following August a new man,
a stranger, moved in and took my place.

You could scarcely start to comprehend
how queer it is, to have your touch
go unfelt, your cries unheard
by your family. Princess!—I called—
Don't let that stranger take your hand!
And—*Em, dear, love, he has no right
to you.*
　　　　　Where did they think I'd gone?
who walked the house all day, all night,
all night. It was far too much
for anyone to endure, and,
hammered by grief one ugly dawn,
I broke. I am still here!—I bawled
from the den—Still here! And no one stirred.

But in time I learned a vicious trick,
a way of gently positing
a breath upon a person's neck
to send an icy run of fear
scampering up the spine—anything,
anything to show them who was near!
. . . Anything, but only to retrieve
some sense that nothing is more
lasting than the love built week by week
for years; I had to believe
again that these were people I'd
give everything, even a life, for.
Then—a second time, and slow—I died.

III

Now I am a shadow of my
former shadow. Seepage of a kind
sets in. Settled concentrations thin.
Amenably—like the smile become
a pond, the pond a mud-lined
bed, from which stems push, pry
and hoist aloft seed-pods that
crack into a sort of grin—
things come almost but not quite
full circle; within the slow
tide of years, water dilutes to light,
light to a distant, eddying hum . . .
In another time, long ago,

I longed for a time when I'd
still felt near enough to recall
the downy scrape of a peach skin
on my tongue, the smell of the sea,
the pull of something resinous.
By turns, I have grown otherwise.
I move with a drift, a drowse that roams
not toward sleep but a clarity
of broadened linkages; it's in
a state wholly too gratified
and patient to be called eagerness
that I submit to a course which homes
outward, and misses nothing at all.

ANGEL

There between the riverbank
and half-submerged tree trunk
it's a kind of alleyway
inviting loiterers—
   in this case, water striders.

Their legs, twice body-length, dent
the surface, but why they don't
sink is a transparent riddle:
the springs of their trampoline
   are nowhere to be seen.

Inches and yet far below, thin
as compass needles, almost, min-
nows flicker through the sun's
tattered netting, circling past
   each other as if lost.

Enter an angel, in
the form of a dragon-
fly, an apparition whose
colouring, were it not real,
   would scarcely be possible:

see him, like a sparkler,
tossing lights upon the water,
surplus greens, reds, milky
blues, and violets blended
   with ebony. Suspended

like a conductor's baton,
he hovers, then goes the one
way no minnow points: straight
up, into that vast solution
   of which he's a concentrate.

MINIATURE

Beneath lilac clusters on a plain
two feet by two, two
long-necked dandelions sway
over a toiling community;
grain by grain,

coppery skin
blazing as if sweat-painted,
the ants amass a sort of pyramid
on Mayan lines: broad
base and truncated cone.

One dandelion
is yellow, is a solar flame
spoking from a green nether rim;
the other grey, a dainty crumb-
cake of a moon.

Soon gusts will shake
this moon and it—no moon at all—
detach a drifting astral
scatter; no sun, the sun cool
and blanch and wear a lunar look;

but under weighted air, noon's
dominion, labourers erect a temple
to this sun and moon, unable
to compass decay, indeed unmindful
of all suns and moons.

11 ASTRONOMICAL RIDDLES

i. The Sun

I am a blinding eye.
I will never relent.
I am magnificent.

I dare them to try.
They hide in the black.
Afraid to attack.

ii. Mercury

I huddle closest to the heat
Yet my back is cold
As ice. I am the most fleet,
If the least bold.

iii. Venus

I am tempestuous, hot and cloudy.
I pay no mind.
Love was intended to be rowdy,
Torrid and blind.

iv. Earth's Moon

I'm an ageing beauty, unique because
It is night not day that betrays my flaws.

v. Earth

I am the spry little
Cell. I am the riddle
Of the chicken or the egg, the miracle of birth.
But for me, none in the heavens would have any worth.

vi. Mars

Chill, frail, friendly . . . I've been misunderstood:
My colour shows a love of warmth, not blood.

vii. Jupiter

The vastest and best am I, the eldest son.
Son in one sense if not the other one . . .
Yet I will be king when his day is done.

viii. An Asteroid

Small, I turn with the great. I feel the same
Call of gravity, though I have no name.

ix. Saturn

Too pretty a ring steals praise from its hand,
Unless the hand be fair enough to wear it.

Around my throat I hook an ivory band.
True beauty is bold; I know my own merit.

x. Uranus and Neptune

We're twins, big-boned boys, pale and overweight.
You mustn't criticize us if we're late.
    It's hard for us to run.
A single lap is an enormous length.
We try not to think, to conserve our strength.
    Sleeping is the most fun.

xi. Pluto

All the others look in; I out.
All the others believe; I doubt.
I stand at the gate of unending Night,
    My fingers on the handle.
Who, when they could have uncountable Light,
    Would settle for a candle?

ODD CARNIVORES

A Venus Flytrap

The humming fly is turned to carrion.
This vegetable's no vegetarian.

A Mosquito

The lady whines, then dines; is slapped and killed;
Yet it's her killer's blood that has been spilled.

MINIMS

A Thumbnail Sketch of Unrequited Love

Your lungs expand; you're smitten—
  She's gnawingly beautiful;

Before long the nail's bitten
  Right down to the cuticle.

The Integers

They serve as stepping stones, neat
  And fitting niches for the mind's feet—
Over a swamp of roots, oddments, monstrous trailing
  Irrationals that never repeat.

Such a Frightening Affair

They've shared now, face to face,
  Maybe a dozen beds—
And still their knees knock heads
  When they embrace.

Trauma

You will carry this suture
  Into the future.
The past never passes.
  It simply amasses.

DAYBREAK

COFFIN POINT
SOUTH CAROLINA

Despite the upward flush, the sky's
kindling from lavender to scarlet,
that first scorched crescent of sun
    lifting from the ocean
still comes as something of a surprise.

The sea, shadowed like the floor
of a forest and matted, apparently,
with a tinder-bed of needles,
    bursts in a moment
with flashfire from horizon to shore.

Inland—meanwhile—the hacked, warning
cry of a rooster sounds, saying,
as unfailingly roosters do: Peril
    is at hand, wake *up*,
wake *up*, this is no ordinary morning!

Now a pause, before the rooster's cry
incites another, and another
even fainter, as one by one
    in their loamy dark
they rise and let uprooted voices fly;

quite soon, by the time their wild
several alarm jangles westward
out of hearing's reach, the sea has
    lapsed into smouldering
patches of fire, and the day seems almost mild.

OLD HAT

It was like you, so considerate a man,
to have your papers in order and to leave
your belongings neat; while compelled to grieve,
we were spared the hard, niggling tasks that can
clutter and spoil grief. Yet not even you
understood how a mere cap on its hook,
companion on those outings you still took,
would hang so heavily now for those who,

like you, would keep a tidy house. We've tried
to sort your things, but where are we to hide
those in which some living threads remain?
What we want is to store such things outside
the slow, spiralling loss of love and pain
that turns you, day by day, into a stranger.

A ROCK WITH A VIEW

MAZATLÁN, MEXICO

Though just a ship as it drags
from the harbour, a change
takes place on the open sea.
With distance its speed declines,
or seems to gradually,
until bit by bit it lags
to a sunny spot and stands still.
Grey and red, what a strange
island it makes!—with its flags
now blooms, pipes and ladders vines,
and smokestack a volcanic hill.

The hill behind me teems
with like abundance: mat
of vegetation plaited
over mat, until it seems
no growth could erupt from that,
and yet the cacti do.
Glabrous, fat, they looked inflated,
like balloons, except where
vines have swarmed into the air
to cover the cacti, too,
and tree-impostors are created.

Lava-like, in turgid waves
from the hilltop, this warm flow
of heavy leafage spills
as if to drown the bay below—
yet never reaches the shore.
The deadly salt air drills
its holes, burns all leaves before
they find the sea; the hill's
green gives way to tumbled stone,
like a row of upthrust graves,
salt-crust edges white as bone.

From a slumped hillside, a ragged
border of greenery
trailing blackened vines,
then piles of cracked boulders
on which the sun shines
brokenly, and an unsteady sea,
waves toppling at the shoulders
to sprawl flat among debris—
no edge that is not jagged,
in all the splintered scenery
no direct, simple lines.

... Lines both sweeping and clear
are found where the ocean
is gently veined: the freighter,
whose sides (though they fence
a swamp of pipes) are sheer;
and beyond, so much greater
the assimilating eye
must now admit the immense
freighter as a toy, the horizon—
that seam of sea and sky
which is the toy ship's destination.

A MICHIGAN GHOST TOWN

It's as though even the ghosts
Have left: no sense of anyone
Lingering here; nothing to weight
The hundreds of poplars—locally
'Popple'—flickering in the light
Breezing of this cool Superior
Noon. Had I not been told
Where to pick out the vined
Roots of a settlement, I might
Have seen no trace at all.
                        It was nothing
But a boomtown, a roof
And a drink, built to last
As long as the timber did, which
Wasn't long. Yet the buzzsaws spun
Mounds and mounds of gold
Dust before they were done.

Up here, back then, it was boom-and-bust;
And after the bust
Sixty, seventy years of thin
Northern sun, of fog turning to snow,
And a tentative, tendrilous
Scrapping with rock and ice,
A re-routing of roots,
A noiseless supplanting as
The popple moved back in—

Trees take the streets.

BETWEEN LEAPS

   Binoculars I'd meant for birds
catch instead, and place an arm's length away,
      a frog
compactly perched on a log that lies
   half in, half out of the river.

   He may be preying, tongue wound to strike,
but to judge from his look of grave languor
      he seems
to be sunning merely. His skin gleams with light
   coming, rebuffed, off the water; his back's

   tawny-spotted, like an elderly hand,
but flank's the crisp, projecting green
      of new
leafage, as if what ran through his veins
   was chlorophyll and he'd

   tapped that vegetal sorcery
which, making light of physical bounds,
      makes food
of light. Given the amplitude of his
   special greenness, it requires no large hop

   of imagination to see him as
the downed trunk's surviving outlet, from which,
      perhaps,
dragged-out years of collapsing roots
   may prove reversible. With a reflection-

   shattering *plop*, a momentary
outbreak of topical, enlarging rings
      that chase
one another frenziedly, the place's spell
   is lifted: the trunk bare, the frog elsewhere.

DUCKWEED

   Where there was a pond there's
Now a floating carpet,
   Gold-butter-green,
   And smooth as pond water.
     The carpet shares

   With those extensive, spare
Cumulus plains one sees by plane
   A false firmness—
   As if only step lightly
     And it would bear

   Your weight; cloud-false, too,
In its suggestion
   Of indwelling light, some
   Deep-deposited radiance.
     Only if you

   Kneel to scrutinize
Its surface closely
   Will you begin to see
   How many mini-lily pads
     Of brad's-head size

   Were needed to transform
The shadowed pool
   Through emanant domain.
   But dip your hands to part
     The duckweed's warm

   Sealing, and here's
A room below: uninviting by
   Nature, and one—chill,
   Dim, jumbled—nobody's
     Entered for years.

ALONG LAKE MICHIGAN

The road abruptly changed to dirt,
Thinned until grasses brushed
The car on both sides, and then
Ended in a loop before the marsh.
We hiked along an arm of land held
Firm by cedars, the lake breaking
Like an ocean on one side,
The rippling, flooded wetlands wide
As a lake on the other.
You found a broad white feather
That could perhaps have been
Converted into a serviceable pen;
We searched for precious stones.
Ahead, brown and white shorebirds,
Probably sandpipers, fled from us
Calling with small chipped voices;
So quick, their matchstick legs
Blurred, like hummingbird wings;
And when they finally stopped,
Their low bodies faded wholly
Into the brown and white rocks.
Later, where the cedars clung
Tight against the lake and crowded out
Our path, we turned towards the marsh,
And some rummaging ducks
Scooted raucously away from us,
Wings striking water repeatedly—
Like a stone sent skipping across—
Before they broke with sudden grace
Into the air. We could hear
Waves falling as we wandered
Through woods that held no breeze,
To a small, harsh clearing where
Three or four fallen trees
Crossed in a tangle. We paused there,
In the sun, and something scary slid
As if across the surface of my eye:
Snakes! Among the logs, we began
To pick them out: fat overlapping coils
Lolling in the light, skin

The colour of sticks; they were hard
To detect, except when in movement.

Along the lake, where a path had slowly
Collapsed the few feet down
To the shore, up-ending little trees until
Their branches tilted into the water,
We found the body of a doe.
The place was quiet, a pond-sized cove
Where the low waves broke slowly,
Lapping up against the body.
Sand had slipped around the legs,
Blanketing the hard hooves,
But trunk and face lay bare, soft,
The tongue limp and grey beneath
Tiny crooked teeth. A wet eyelash, left
Over an eye picked clean to the bone,
Seemed a tawdry, artificial touch.
I looked for bullets, but found no holes,
Blood, nothing. The massive body lay
Fetid and undisturbed, like a mariner's
Daydream beached up in a storm:
A strange tawny sea-creature . . .
I fanned away the flies that speckled
The blond flank, and we saw them hover,
Land, and then resume their tracking.
We held hands, kneeling beside the body
As if we could impart a gift
Of movement: possible here, on a day
When we'd seen sticks slither
And stones take flight, for this
Animal to rise at our whispering and shake
Sleep from its sandy coat. We watched
The clear waves curl, then break
Against the chest like a heartbeat.

BIRCHES

    Generously overgrown,
it's still a kind of clearing:
the sunlight's different here
above the fern bed, somehow
brighter and gentler at once
as birches draw the presence
of clouds down into the forest.

    While in this light they suggest
(the narrow limbs, and fair skin
peeling as if with sunburn)
something young and feminine,
they will on an afternoon
black with storm evoke that soon-
to-thunder first stroke of lightning.

    In composing complements
to the stolid pine, the sun-
siphoning birches vary
not merely with the seasons
but with the minute hourly
unravellings of the day,
freshly hopeful at dawn in their

    tattered but immaculate
bandages and at dusk war-
painted, trunks smeared a savage
red; they are becomingly
multiform and a forest
that boasts even a modest
stand of birch maintains its daily

    log of weather conditions
and a hinted timelessness—
as when, given the right light,
birches from their swampy pool
of ferns lift tall saurian
necks to browse, small heads unseen,
in the overhanging leafage.

ADDITIONAL BATS

Nightfall loosens them from the rocks
   And trees to which like mushrooms
They fasten. Against the clearing's still-
   lavender sky, dissolving in

And out of sight as fish will
   Under the glinting and smoky
Lid of a stream, the bats
   Pull to their swarm additional bats.

Theirs seems a gimpy flight, crude
   Aerial gallop, yet they live
By hunting on the wing—swoop to strain
   The quick night air for food—

As an outflung vision, surer
   Far than sight, sounds the treetops
At clearing's edge, the outcrops
   Of stone, the ferns, the dense, standing

Water in the overhung ditch,
   And returns as rumpled echoes to
Ears that map the field according to
   Its shifting, imperfect pitch.

A QUILLED QUILT, A NEEDLE BED

Under the longleaf pines
The curved, foot-long needles have
Woven a thatchwork quilt—threads,
Not patches, windfall millions
Looped and overlapped to make
The softest of needle beds.

The day's turned hot, the air
Coiling around the always
Cool scent of pine. As if lit
From below, a radiance
Milder yet more clement than
The sun's, the forest-carpet

Glows. It's a kind of pelt:
Thick as a bear's, tawny like
A bobcat's, more wonderful
Than both—a maize labyrinth
Spiralling down through tiny
Chinks to a caked, vegetal

Ferment where the needles
Crumble and blacken. And still
The mazing continues . . . whorls
Within whorls, the downscaling
Yet-perfect intricacies
Of lichens, seeds, and crystals.

CANOEING AT NIGHT

I

Water pulled on wood at first
And muscles bunched. We struck
The bank once, with dull solidity.
Spinning free, we turned a wide arc,
Sliding through forest into forest,
Changes that brought no change. Cold,
Cramping, we wanted more than this.
We worked against ourselves,
Shoveling up water that dropped away,
Digging holes in the river
That filled behind us.
We thought of the lamp
Hung downstream on a limb.
Stop, it meant, and that
Is what we wanted.

II

Later we get our timing back.
Clapping bats come down to us,
Sounding us out. And though
Not quite sure of the river,
We steer for the centre
And catch the cold drift of it.
We wait for something: a snapping
Of fish, a rustling in the grass;
We wait to face a silver animal
Rapt in its own reflection.
Listening straight into the woods,
We try to lose all other
Noises—the wrinkling of water
Or our own steady breathing.

III

Here, the river is deeper. The moon
Climbs up over the woods. We move
Fast, and in this new light
It is all white water.
Smoothly opening up to us,
The river falls forward;
Trees swing by, bobbing,
As if they float on water.
You and I, we take the bends together,
One good turn on another, moving
Along to where our knot of light
Lies unravelled in the water.

AN EXPANDED WANT AD

          Rent—cttge Pig Riv
          3 bdrm stove fridge
          20 acr—lovely view

    Although it's true
a few screens are torn and various
uninvited types may flutter through,
    some of them to bite you,

    and true the floors
buckle and sag like a garden ploughed
by moles, which makes the shaky chairs
    seem shakier, and the bedroom doors

    refuse to close
(you'll have three bright bedrooms—and a fine
kitchen, a living room with fireplace,
    and bath with shower hose),

    there's a good view
of the Pigeon, a river that carries
more than its share of sunny jewellery,
    for days here are mostly blue,

    and nights so clear
and deep that in a roadside puddle
you can spot the wobbly flashlight flare
    of even a minuscule star.

    The jolting road,
two muddy ruts, flanks a weedy fan
that slithers against the underside
    of a car, then rises unbowed,

    but better still,
go on foot—though this means mosquitoes—
and stop at the overgrown sawmill,
    with its fragrant wood-chip pile,

  and, stooping, enter
that shack the length of a compact car
where two loggers outbraved the bitter
  sting of a Michigan winter.

  The room is dim,
spider-strung; you'll sense the whittled lives
they led—how plain, pure, and coldly grim
  the long months were to them . . .

  Just a short ways
up the road you'll come to a birch clump
which on all overcast mornings glows
  with a cumulus whiteness

  and in the brief
light after sunset holds a comely
allusive blush—a mix that's one half
  modesty, the other mischief.

  While if you hike
to where the road feeds a wider road
you'll find a mailbox above a choke
  of weeds, leaning on its stake;

  it looks disowned,
worthless, but will keep your letters dry
though its broken door trails to the ground
  like the tongue of a panting hound.

  Venture across
this wider road to reach a pasture,
whose three horses confirm that 'the grass
  is always greener' applies

  to them as well:
offered shoots from your side of the fence,
they'll joggle forward to inhale
  a verdant airy handful,

    and will emit
low shivering snorts of joy, and will—
while you feed them—show no appetite
    for the grass growing at their feet.

    Now, it may happen
the first nights you'll feel an odd unease,
not lessened by the moth's crazed tapping
    at the glass; and later, sleeping

    unsteadily,
as bullfrogs hurl harsh gravelly notes
from slingshot throats, you may wonder why
    you ever left the city.

    Should this occur,
think of the creatures you've not yet glimpsed,
the owl and woodchuck and tense-necked deer
    you'll meet if you remain here;

    remember, too,
morning's flashy gift—for when day breaks
it mends all wrongs by offering you
    drenched fields, nearly drowned in dew.

HUNDREDS OF FIREFLIES

Sky yet violet,
shadows collecting
under the trees

and first stars wan
as night birches, the fireflies
begin: from the first,

the night belongs
to them.   Darkness brightens
them: from our screened porch

we watch their blinkings
sharpen: three, four of them
lighten nightfall of all

solemnity; ten or twelve
and the eyes are led
endlessly astray;

and in deeper night
it's twenty, fifty, more—a number
beyond simple reckoning—

and still they keep
coming.   No winter
surpasses the flash

of their storm, no spring
their startling growth.   Expanding
to contain them, the night fills

with their soundless poppings,
hundreds of fireflies,
each arhythmic light a trinket

to entice some wayward mate
into the joined darkness
of propagation . . .

So it's as wooers they come
bumbling to the cottage screens
to illumine palely, eerily

our faces, and but a creature's
prime, combinatory urge
erects constellations brighter,

nearer than the heavens
will ever be.
              Merely
to watch, and say nothing,

gratefully,
is what is best, is
what we needed.
                 For we've seen

stars enough tonight
to hold us through a year
of city living—

lengthening fall nights,
opened trees and the rosy
murk of shopping plazas;

and skies greyly gathering snow,
and the moon of crusted snow,
and marshy April skies clogged

with sediment . . . until the silent
drift of summer through the trees
signals us, drawn too by light,

to another brief firefly season.

THE RETURN TO A CABIN

Cool suddenly,
your first night, and so queer
at once to discover

how many things
you'd forgotten or concealed:
the forest thickening and the wild

frantic ticking in the weeds
like a thousand racing clocks
and the loose packs

of what could be birds
gathering over the river but
for their peculiar, skidding flight;

in a spare, wooden room
that seems with the nightfall
to have changed its smell

you move and even think
warily, new noises sinking in
by way of your prickled skin . . .

You retained the joys
of a sunset here—cloud
and birch-clump dyed

the same watery pink
and the day's last light
bundled off by the river—but not

the succeeding fright
which catches like a burr
in the chest, threatening to tear,

and nothing of how a sky
so overrun by stars
can chase a person indoors

and nothing of the frenzied
strength of moths—just like a man's
knock—knocking on the windowpanes.

TWO SUMMER JOBS

I. *Tennis Instructor, 1971*

Transformed: the high school graduate, now
himself a teacher for the city.
Not sure who my students are, or how
exactly a tennis class is run,
I show up an hour ahead of time.
Odd: nobody here. But one by one
they appear and—and they're all women!
Maddeningly shy, the truth is I'm
more alarmed than pleased at this, although
a number of them are pretty,
and one, Mrs Shores, extremely so.

Mine's a small yet adequate domain.
Three mornings a week I hold court
on two courts beside the railroad track—
giving, to those I can, assistance,
and verbally patting on the back
the irretrievably maladroit
whose shots are always rocketing
the fence. Occasionally a train
hurtling to or from Detroit
rumbles through, erasing everything
before it fades into the distance.

Distant but surreally vast,
exclusive, quick to take offence,
the 'Big H', Harvard, which only last
April accepted me, now conspires
(my latest crazy daydream runs)
to bar me from settling in a dorm
because I typed 'No class presidents,
please' on my roommate selection form.
Just as I'm lunging toward the ball,
a sniping voice within inquires,
'What will happen in the fall?'

The days are changeless, but the weeks pass,
edging me closer to fall, and school.
Mrs Shores, the day of our last class,
gives a party on her patio,
where I'm handed a glass-bottom mug
—surprise!—engraved with my name.
Beer's offered; I'm too proud to confess
I hate the stuff. It's hot as a blow-
torch now, and not yet noon. The first slug
of Stroh's goes down in a cool
wash of cleansing bitterness.

The party warms up, visibly. Ice
crackles in the drinks. I'm nonplussed
when Mrs Binstock unfolds a tale
which—though nothing you shouldn't say
among men—is not exactly nice.
My face, which lets me down without fail
at such times, blushes. They laugh at me.
Then, and this is odd, I am discussed
in a fond but distant-seeming way,
as if I were no longer here.
The ghost accepts another beer.

Mrs Dow speaks of a friend's friend's son
who committed suicide after
his first Harvard exam. A lighter
flares beside me, and cigarette smoke
crowds the air. 'Teacher don't allow
any smoking.' Freshened laughter
greets sad Mrs Klein's unlikely quip.
Then, from Mrs Shores: 'What kind of writer
do you want to be?' How, how, how
did she ever draw from me my one
most private wish? I'm tempted to joke,

but a stilled politeness in the air
and the depths of her dark handsome eyes
forbid it. Yet when I stumblingly
begin a pained, self-conscious reply
she is mercifully there
to cut me off; conversation drifts
lightly away, as once more I
find myself taking shelter in
something that soothes as it puzzles me—
a solicitude that's graceful, wise,
and impenetrably feminine.

I drain my mug. A white film adheres
to the glass bottom, and then bursts:
disclosing these my students seated
around me in the Michigan sun,
the last of our lessons completed.
Wobbly I rise, drunk with success
(successfully having drunk four beers!),
and wave goodbye—but forget the press
to my racket. I'm called back amid
much laughter. Once more I gravely bid
them all farewell: So long. It's been fun.

. . . And what a day this is! The air
humming in my ears, the sun stroking
overheads in the treetops! Now
a second film breaks, revealing how
the light-drinking leaves, the houses, cars,
power lines, a peeling wooden fence
and the pavement's constelled stars
are a network, supple and immense,
and all linked to distant Mrs Shores,
who calls—but surely she is joking—
'Never forget: the world is yours.'

II. Law Clerk, 1979

My fingers having checked and re-checked my tie,
I'm at ease—or nearly so. We're lunching high
over Manhattan, a hundred floors above
streets new to me still. He asks whether I

find the work 'exciting'. Behind him a buffet
tastefully boasting shrimp, squid salad, pâté,
beef, chicken, cheeses, and some good marinated
mushrooms, calls me to come boyishly away

and fill my plate a second time. And I'd love
another beer. I think he thinks that one's enough.
'Exciting? Very'—which is not untrue.
'Best of all'—I'm speaking off the (starchy) cuff–

'I liked the document search in Tennessee.'
Indeed, I did. How strange, how fine to be
a someone someone flies a thousand miles
to analyse ancient business files! Now he—

but who is he? A *partner*, first of all,
by which is meant no confederate or pal
of mine, but a star in the firm's firmament.
He's kind, though, funny, and lunch is going well

enough—the conversation light, the view vast
beyond my furthest hopes. The kid's arrived at last:
not just New York, but New York at the top.
Just think of all the noontime views that passed

into the void because I wasn't here! Think
of the elevated wines I never drank
in this very room! The tortes I failed to eat!
—Lunch here is money in the memory bank.

Why, then, wishing I were somewhere else? Why
does my glance drift sidelongingly, my mind stray
from his fatherly banter? When will I shake
this shakiness? It's worse at night. I sometimes stay

late at the office. The place starts thinning out
by six; cleaning women, outfitted to fight
their bosses' daily disarray, marshal vacuums,
trashbins, brooms. Their leaving leaves me free to write,

or to try, as the city underfoot
starts breathing visibly, bubbles of light,
hundreds and hundreds, a champagne glitter
promising love and—more—a distant, delicate

loveliness. *Here* is inspiration. Yet the clock
clicks; my mind does not. Could this be 'writer's block',
nothing but that ailment which, like tennis elbow,
raises its victim's status? Yet it's no joke,

this scooped-out feeling, a sense that language
will never span the gap within. The Brooklyn Bridge,
trafficking in cars and literary ghosts,
shimmers mockingly below. I can't budge

the block; thwarted, I inch instead toward parody,
Keats' 'On the Grasshopper and Cricket' to be
wittily urbanized as 'The Snowplough
and the Lawnmower'; I'll set 'The poetry

of earth is never dead' upon its head.
And yet, though I have the title, and the thread
of a joke as a starter's cord, 'Snowplough' will not
start: some mechanical failure under the hood.

In a later, hopeless project Shakespeare
writes in a fancy bar—'To beer or not to beer'
and 'The Singapore Slings and Sombreros
cost an outrageous fortune.' I'm going nowhere . . .

Most nights, the air's sticky. Too hot to jog,
I take myself out for a walk, like a dog,
once round the block. Inside, endlessly, my
electric fan rustles like a paper bag;

and armed with a borrowed book called *Parodies*,
I rifle my old English 10 anthologies
in search of targets. It seemed this would be simple
but it's not. And I'm hot. And the nights pass

slowly. Then: a new month: still stuck, parodies lost,
when, wolfing lamb at lunch, I find I've crossed
Cinderella's fable (a cleaning woman swept
like me into moneyed worlds) with—Robert Frost.

'Whose shoe this is I need to know.
Throughout the countryside I'll go
In search of one whose gaze is clear,
Whose royal skin is white as snow.'

Now *this* is simple, stanzas dropping into place,
and while I couldn't say precisely what it is
I'd like to say, just writing quickly is enough.
And the last stanza is, I think, quite nice:

'And if she's lost, I'll settle cheap—
A helpmate from the common heap,
Some kitchenmaid or chimneysweep,
Some kitchenmaid or chimneysweep.'

What now?—next? Will the impasse pass? After work,
I'm roundabouting home through Central Park
when a voice cuts short all questions. *'Bradford.'*
It sounds like someone I hope it isn't.' '. . . Mark.'

He's wearing jeans and a work-shirt with a rip
in the neck, whereas I'm caught in the trap-
pings of a Wall Street lawyer. As we lob our
pleasantries across the Sartorial Gap

he studies me. Mark's a poet too, if you take
the thought for the deed—but who am I to talk?
At Harvard, hardly friends, we were nonetheless
drawn together by a fiercely sophomoric

contest: my-potential's-bigger-than-yours.
He's just in for the day, he quickly offers,
as if this were a kind of feat. City living
taints the artist's soul—he's suggesting of course—

which is his old, still tiresome refrain. So why
do I yet feel some need to justify
myself to him, who, he tells me, moved to a farm,
makes pots (a bad sign) and (I'm sure) lives high

on Daddy's bucks. His dad makes pots and pots
of money in securities—but let's
not hear me griping at the rich while wearing
one of my two two-hundred-dollar suits.

Mark draws from a knapsack the books he's bought—
Pound, Lawrence, Durrell (I thought he was out),
Smart and Clare (safer choices, both being mad)
and a surprising, handsome *Rubaiyat*.

Mark asks about my job. He has me twice
repeat my salary, each time bulging his eyes
in sham barefaced amazement. Later, alone
and gleefully free to wage my wars in peace,

I derail a quatrain (striking at that band
of Harvard potters who'd 'live off the land'
a summer or two before going on
for MBA's, just as the parents planned):

'A Book of Verses underneath the Bough,
A Jug of Wine, a Loaf of Bread, and Thou-
sands in the Bank; fleeting though Riches be,
And powerless, They comfort anyhow.'

Yes . . . And all at once, summer's nearly through.
I return *Parodies*, a week overdue.
And I'm asked to join the firm, beginning next year,
with four months to decide . . . Oftener now

I linger at work, to watch how the setting sun
at once sharpens and softens the skyline;
sometimes—the better for being rare—the dusk-light's
perfect and, while occupied toy boats twine

the Hudson with long, unravelling wakes,
the sun buffs hundreds of windows, reglazes bricks,
ruddies a plane's belly like a robin's,
and seems to free us from billable time, from stocks

and bonds (both words a pun, ironically,
on hand-fetters), leases, estate taxes, proxy
fights, adverse parties, complainants, claimants,
motions to suppress, to enjoin, to quash, oxy-

moronic lengthy briefs, and the whole courtly game
of claim and counterclaim; seems to say we come
through drudgery to glory . . . Look—down there! Wall
Street's turned to gold at last! And there are some

silver nights of emptied offices, raindrops
washing out the glue on those envelopes
in which memories are sealed and the entire
cleared distances offered up, all the old hopes

intact, as if nothing's been mislaid. This obscure
sense that one's past is safely banked somewhere
finds confirmation each time the recumbent
city, touched by darkness, begins to stir

and with a sufferance that's nearly heartbreaking
undergoes a pane by pane awakening
until just as fresh, as sparklingly replete
as last night, or any night before: *not a thing*

is lost. The frail headlights drift, as white as snow
it's fair to say. I'll leave here soon, for good. I know
'for good' is for the better, in some ways, and know
I'll be ready to leave. Or nearly so.

TWO SUSPENSIONS
AGAINST A BLACKTOP BACKDROP

    Straight up noon, I watch a toad
       —dusty, huge—cross a blacktop road
    by hops and halts; landing each
       time like a splattered
egg, he regathers, heavily pauses
    in the baking sun, and heaves
aloft again, again until he makes
    the road's shoulder, come
       to rest finally under some
dusty asparagus leaves.

    Next—and from nowhere,
       from right out of the air—
       quick as thought
       drops a damselfly,
the wings that keep
    her motionless an icy blur
of motion . . . Each at each appeared
    to peer: he maybe held
       by the sun-enamelled
emerald stickpin of her

    spare torso; she,
       by a stolidity
so extreme it looks
       accomplished, a dumb but deep-
rooted contentment. Perhaps,
    of course, this choice encounter
wasn't one and their gazes
    never met; yet they seemed to,
       at least for a few
suspensive seconds that were—

were, obscurely, reminiscent of
   a web I'd found just above
my head that same summer, which,
   metaphor for memory
turned selfless, by a trick
of the light had altogether
vanished, yielding to the eye
   but what incidence had blown there:
      some seeds, needles, threadbare
leaves, a curled grey feather—

were, surely, irresistible grist
   for the fabulist,
who might well conclude
   that each, true to the instant's
instance, as it urged the
resolution of mind and mass,
had felt the other's opposed
   appeals, and however much
      could pass between two such
contrary creatures indeed did pass.

THE BURIED GRAVES

From the pier, at dusk, the dim
    Billowing arms of kelp
Seem the tops of trees, as though
    Not long ago
A summer wood stood here, before a dam
    Was built, a valley flooded.

Such a forest would release
    Its colour only slowly,
And the leafy branches sway, as they'd
    More lightly swayed
Under a less distant sun and far less
    Even weather. Now, deeper down,

Those glimmers of coral might
    Be the lots of some hard-luck
Town, or—depositing on the dead
    A second bed—
A submerged cemetery. . . . To this mute,
    Envisioned, birdless wood would

Come a kind of autumn, a tame
    Sea-season, with foliage tumbling
Through a weighty, trancelike fall;
    And come, as well,
Soon in the emptying fullness of time,
    A mild but an endless winter.

AN ACTOR PLAYS A TRUMPET

        What comes through
in this rooftop conclusion to an old movie
     in which somebody who
clearly doesn't know how to play it
picks up a banged-up trumpet
    to play against a light-hung screen
      meant to represent
  a metropolitan skyline

        is some sense
of the soaring and transformative strength
     of jazz. When he plants
his bandaged shoes, cocks his boyish profile
and lifts the horn to ride a gorgeous roll
    of dubbed spontaneity, the effect is (despite
      that bogus clothesline at
  his back, with its one limp sheet)

        persuasive:
those high, ramping notes speak of daring,
     the flutter-throated vibrato of
diffidence, and the whole of unformed
invention, wound yet in the horn's warmed-
    up cerebric densities. Indeed, so fine
      is the music, even his
  acting's better for it and as the camera tracks in

        on the sure
kiss at the tiny mouthpiece, you might
     almost believe that here
is a man whose upper lip burns, night
after night, in the effort
    to make unpremeditation look
      easy. Although he's
  turning his back on the city, the music

     is a gift
to its boxed-in inhabitants: the loose,
  looping melodies waft
over the roof's edge, falling,
and, in falling, joining
  that collected world of objects you've watched
    falling on film—all
the briefcases and rifles and bottles pitched

     from tower
and cliff-top, the beribboned packets
  of love-letters lofted over
the rails of ocean liners, the open buckets
of paint, the key rings and miner's flashlights,
  the flying anvils and leather-upholstered
    convertibles and sun
hats and muddied sacks of gold. . . . Gold

     as the moon
ought to be, the pounded streets, the lumpen
  heart that weights a man,
stooping his shoulders—just that fleeting,
flyaway colour are the tones tonight lighting
  off his horn. And when a slow
    coldness blows in, a gold-
to-blue harmonic shift, oh

     he's dying
up there with the fit sweetness of it,
  digging hard, as with a shovel, going
deep for the ultimate, most intimate
strain in his chest. The multi-storied, tight-
  plotted metropolis at his feet,
    coruscating all the more
for the yearnings he lays upon it,

     would topple
if he hurled his trumpet at it.

DAINTIES: A SUITE

I. Recollections of an Irish Daybreak

Dawn in its high-
flung overtones
alights upon
the hilltops first,
descending by
warming degrees
slopes still nearer
silver than green
as the sun lifts
and the sea takes
on then loses
its scumbling blue,
lavender, rose
and peach glazes;

sprung aerial
arousals, big
bulging reaches'
enkindlings come
seasonably
down to grounded
unveilings that
lighten but lend
no colour to
all of the grey
stone walls that spill
with the smoothed trends
of streams down each
responsive hill.

And while, up close,
these walls are seen
as nothing more
than reject moons,
or misshapen
skulls of a lax,
superseded
race that left in
terms of remains
nothing but its
bones, they display
to someone at
a sufficient
distance—to, say,

a young man perched
commandingly
on a boulder
whose barnacle-
gripped, weed-strung base
the sea rinses—
all of the live,
slung fluency
of spider's thread.
How handsomely
from his select
vantage (with a
zigzag jigsaw
puzzle effect)

II. Rabbits: A Valentine

the whole terrain
has come to be
overlain by
one extended
web, in whose most
ample, fertile
interstices
fields are tended,
cattle fatten,
chimneys project
their indolent
and indirect
assault upon
the firmament.

Deliberate
on the rabbit,
who if what you
hear is half true
has found the way
to inhabit
a world without
elaborate
courtship, yet one
flushed with piquant
concupiscent
satisfaction,
a world whose slack
meadowed moments
sit suspended
between frequent
bouts of rabid
raptured action . . .
males of splendid
near-heroic
virility,
females of a
commensurate,
magnificent
fertility.

Ponder this shy
but quite able
go-get-'er, for
whom even sex
is not complex,
who meets and mates,
and keeps no count
but sees the flesh-
of-his-flesh both
diversify
and multiply;
who does not tire
for long, and with
the great outdoors
as his table
banquets on fresh
greens as he waits
for the desire
to mount to mount.

Consider this
suitor of sorts
who advocates
a direct style,
who's sharp on fun-
damentals and
in a twinkling,
his little heart
kicking, is hard
at it; who gets
and forgets while
composing no
explanations,
damnations, grand
pleadings or vows—
disengages
and instantly
begins to browse,
lifting to all
eyes his eyes (oh,
those lovable
black bunny eyes!)
innocent and
intelligent.

III. In a Bonsai Nursery

Nearly nothing
in Nature so
spirits the eye
off—but off by
way of in—to
unveil detail
as minimal
as it's recep-
tive to as does
this more than true-

to-life, living
family of
diminutive
replicas of
themselves, whose pin-
point blossomings
and punctual
leaf-losses, whose
every nubbled
knob and fissure,

knot-imploded
distension and
deep, thematic
torsion reproach
our recognized
but unrenounced
confusion of
size with grandeur.

These pondered, hand-
won triumphs of
containment, come,
tentatively,
of earth-toughened
fingers, father
to son, and on
to son, so long
as the branches
hold on each side,

bid us enter-
tain notions of
days whose hours are
shorter than ours
(shrunken, misted,
mossed-in seasons,
amassed in hard-
pressed heartwood rings) . . .
and enter, please,
a forest where

sun, planets, stars,
and our little
still-swollen moon
are brought, though yet
unreachable,
nearer the roofs
of the trim, smoke-
puffing houses.

A STUFFED TORTOISE

Inwardly re-outfitted over a century ago
according to the handwritten, yellow
three-by-five directly below
the lunging neck, he is, among this petrified
   menagerie, just as once in life,

the oldest of animals. The armadillo
beside him, the Manx cat, the dartlike row
of birds along the wall, all look as though
they never were alive, but whoever re-posed
   our tortoise attended to that

tension which makes him—with the frog and fox—so
didactically adaptable: Who can resist the slow-
paced, cumulative humour of this low-
profiled plodder, who somehow sweeps
   the big races, speaks volumes by example only,

and, fetchingly shy, zeroes inward at any show
of attention—and yet whose narrow,
near-panicky glance is that of some desperado
on the lam? The neck strains, *forward,*
   as if that tough, undersized head

yearned to outstrip its ponderous cargo.
—The time's not ripe for that? If so, the true
burden on his back may be years which offer no
movement casual or quick enough to escape
   a painstaking, on-the-spot review.

MINIMS

Manifest Destiny

Now if, somehow, offered a brand-new New
World, an endless, arable *tabula rasa*,
Wouldn't we dedicate that one, too, to
The billboard, the smokestack, the shopping plaza?

That Trojan Horse

It pretty much stinks,
though it may be only human—
the way Man looks at Woman
and secretly thinks,
You've got to believe
it's better to give than to receive.

The Fame Train

The season's major talents are
Roaring up the track.
You can hear them coming: clique
Claque, clique claque.

Post-Coitum Tristesse: A Sonnet

Why
do
you
sigh,
roar,
fall,
all
for
some
hum-
drum
come
—mm?
Hm . . .

Freudian Slip

With this turnabout
a wild brain-child
is beguiled
out;

when at last the wits
relent, the self
reveals its-
elf.

SEAHORSES

    Kin to all kinds
Of fancied hybrids—minotaur
    And wyvern, cockatrice,
Kyrin and griffin—this
Monkey-tailed, dragon-chested
    Prankish twist of whimsy
Outshines that whole composited
Menagerie, for this sequined
    Equine wonder, howsoever
        Improbably,

    Quite palpably
Exists! Within his moted
    Medium, tail loosely laced
Round the living hitching post
Of a coral twig, he feeds at leisure
    As befits a mild, compromising
Creature with no arms of defence
Save that of, in his knobby
    Sparsity, appearing
        Unappetizing.

    Like that chess piece
He so resembles, he glides
    With a forking, oblique
Efficiency, the winglike
Fins behind his ears aflutter;
    And like that lone
Unmastered steed to whom
The word-weary everywhere
    Look for replenishment—
        That is to say, our own

       Like-winged, light-winged
Pegasus—he can be taken
   As an embodiment
Of the obscure fount
And unaccountable buoyancy
   Of artistic inspiration.
Yet defined by neither,
Finally, by nothing afloat
   On the long, circulating
      Seas of creation,

   Is this mailed male
Who bears in his own brood pouch
   A female's transferred conceptions,
And seems to move (those fins
By turns transparent) through
   Telekinetic promptings, while his
Turreted, nonsynchronous
Eyes are taking in two
   Views at once. How appropriate
      That gaze of his is—

   For he conveys
A sense of living at least two
   Simultaneous lives, of always
Having a mucilaginous
If metaphorical foot
   Planted in a neighbouring, renum-
bered dimension, one whose
Dim-sensed presence releases our
   Ineffable but hopeful
      Yearnings for some

    Further release.
In his otherworldliness
    He heartens us. . . . If there's to be
Any egress for you and me
From the straitening domain
    Of the plausible, what course
More likely than astride the plated
Shoulders of this shimmering
    Upright swimmer, this
        Waterbound winged horse?

A NOISY SLEEPER

I. 1958

The noisy sleeper
in the other room is my
Grandfather whose snores go up & down
up & down like a zipper. Deeper

deeper for the dark
his big breathing climbs
& slips away
like the moon like the day

like Cinny who I so
much wanted to stay
here with me in a bed too big
for me. But Cinny when I let her go

was gone
on her clicking toes
in blackness with the thin slits
open on her black nose

and not a shiver in her chest
for what out there just might
be waiting. She lies at ease I know
on a floor in the night

body curled completely
in the safety of a ring
in whose fur centre her head
fits neatly.

In his desk for luck he keeps
an Indian head
penny with the date
he was born which is 1898.

He promised he will look
for one for luck for me
which is 1953.
Whatever

could be that's wrong
what is needed I know
is to be watchful to be strong
simply

though such breathing's far
too big for this house in which
he & I together are
sleeping and I do not sleep.

II. 1983

    Recalling now
From the subsiding brink
Of earliest memory
The night-sounds of that man,
My grandfather, is to see
How even at age five one can
Accept reassurances as though
They were believable while
Darkly continuing to think
Things over—to see how
Soon the mind learns to reconcile
Itself to a complex ignorance,
As one begins to know

    One does not know.
Now whatever that unnamed
Crisis actually was which placed me
In that giant's bed that night
(Illness in the family?
Some remote, unheard-of fight?
Or, likelier, a disaster lifted
From the blaze of a small boy's inflamed
Imagination . . .) it passed
Much as night passes into dawn,
Unobserved and at last,
Leaving no trace as it drifted
Wholly out of mind. Gone—

Like the existence
Of all others in that house. No doubt
My grandmother was there, too,
Sleeping or, like me, pretending
To sleep, but I don't recall
Her presence, or anyone who
Played with me that day, or what fell out
The next. No, in memory
It's simply two people all
Alone, my grandfather and me,
Bound across the distance
Of a night that rises
And falls and has no ending.

   But given all
Memory's shortcomings, one still must
Marvel at its power to restore
The feel of that small boy's fears,
Or the way it can take an old man
Dead now some twenty years
And hold him up close enough
To overhear the rise and fall
Of his slow breathing, just
As though his were once more
The sort of sleep from which—broken
By ruminative snorts, gruff
Assentive gasps—he could be woken.

FLOATING LIGHT IN TOKYO

Having lost track of the time in your own
country, how long you've been up, how little
you slept on the plane, but finding yourself alone
in a small room in an enormous city

you take the elevator down to the dim
lobby and feeling just like a criminal slip
out for a walk beside the moated rim
of the Imperial Palace. It's late—

even the packed, desperate thoroughfares
of Central Tokyo are all but deserted.
Vistas have opened up, and the air's
cooled a bit at last. You can hear

a few horns honking in the distance,
also a heavy truck which, meeting
strong internal resistance,
manfully strains and strains as it climbs

into gear and rumbles off. Such sounds
deepen rather than deplete the sensation
of an enchanted spell of sleep that extends
over miles and millions. Yet it's you

who's about to awaken, as a bend in the moat
reveals a vision—enchanted, too—
of frenzy: a jewelled inner city afloat
in light, the mad neon dazzle of the Ginza....

The neon blazes cleanly in the old moat.
Lights on lights are overlaid in repeated
applications which soothe somewhat
a staggered, jet-lagged brain that longs

to rest yet somehow can't; for they fill
the mind as dreams do, these flourishing
ribbons on the ebony flux, the spill
of moons, keys and horns, the many-petalled rose

and amber and azure blooms that flare
and fade, flare and fade in rocking
even rhythms. How pleasing they are!—
these emblems from a Halloween magician's cape,

these colours selected for brightness alone,
recalling jars of fingerpaint on the low shelves
of a primary classroom. With regret, then,
you note an approaching duck, whose wake shivers

all reflections; and it hurts a little
to watch the neat incision being cut, the plush
collapse begin as the first nudging ripple
swings outwards. Yet as the duck, in passing,

transforms into a swan, the shapely *S*
of the neck lit in sudden fluorescent profile,
and familiar designs begin to coalesce
within the moat, which soon again will reflect

composedly, you'll grant that while the static
glaze was restful, welcome is this
queen of birds with the sea-serpentine neck,
who trails behind her such thrilling rubble.

HESITANCY

    For a start here's hesitancy
played on a breezy afternoon
    at the Kyoto Zoo by an
ostrich met with the offer
    of a pretzel: a pink two-toed
stalking to the fence, there to pin
    upon the quailing child
    the enlarged, enraged glare
of the born disciplinarian,
while all the while the neck's
spiral tube's atremble,
    for the bird, too, is fearful. . . .

    Through hesitancy we are placed
in kinship with the scarred rat
    as it hungrily sniffs at
the broken cellar window;
    elsewhere, with the chary
candy-striped spider as
    with an evenhanded
    sinister dexterity
it sidesteps fatefully
toward that wobble in the web
that may mean prey, or
    may mean predator.

    A joint appeal in all
things subject to a contrary
    pull—as in the very
faint, loose-lipped whistle
    of a warming kettle, or that
blackened buried moment when
    a cloudburst's certain
    but still nothing, not a drop,
    spills, or the hairline
fissure's inchmeal venture
down the flume's granite wall—
    links our comical, our pretzel-

       necked ostrich, so far
from its home, with the rupturing
       perilous push of a king-
       side pawn: a mere one-square
       advance along the board's
periphery, and yet a move
       hazarded only upon
         long mulling within
       the miniaturized viscera
of a grandmaster computer.
For pause links with pause,
       or will at least for those

       yearning to feel that these
things, too, go with some minimal
       reluctance, don't just tumble
     —so much deadweight cargo—
       down and down in projectable
collisions, forever locked
       in the straitened chute
         of strict causality . . . but know
       in every pressing second
second thoughts, and a doubt
turned wishful: *if we are not free,*
       we would like to be.

IN MINAKO WADA'S HOUSE

In old Minako Wada's house
Everything has its place,
And mostly out of sight:
    Bedding folded away
    All day, brought down
    From the shelf at night,

Tea things underneath
Low tea table and tablecloth—
And sliding screen doors,
    Landscape-painted, that hide
    Her clothes inside a wash
    Of mountains. Here, the floors

Are a clean-fitting mosaic,
Mats of a texture like
A broom's; and in a niche
    In the tearoom wall
    Is a shrine to all of her
    Ancestors, before which

She sets each day
A doll-sized cup of tea,
A doll-sized bowl of rice.
    She keeps a glass jar
    Of crickets that are fed fish
    Shavings, an eggplant slice,

And whose hushed chorus,
Like the drowsy toss
Of a baby's rattle, moves in
    On so tranquil a song
    It's soon no longer heard.
    The walls are thin

In Minako Wada's little house,
Open to every lifting voice
On the street—by day, the cries
    Of the children, at night
  Those excited, sweet,
  Reiterated goodbyes

  Of men full of beer who now
Must hurry home. Just to
Wake in the night inside this nest,
    Late, the street asleep (day done,
  Day not yet begun), is what
  Perhaps she loves best.

THE TIGERS OF NANZEN-JI

    These light-footed, celebrated
        cats, created
on gold-leaf screens by a man
    who'd never seen a tiger
        (there were none in Japan),
who worked, as he'd been taught,
from pelts, and from paintings brought
    from distant, brilliant China,

    wander an extraordinary
        maze whose very
air's alive, alit with breeze-
    borne inebriants. It's a place
        of tumbled boundaries
and whetted penchants, in which
big-chested brutes whose eyes are rich
    outsize eggs of burnished gold,

    whose coats are cloudy, glowing
        masses flowing
behind an emerald palisade
    of bamboo and the row
        of darker palings made
by their own sable bands, glide
fatefully in the failing light, wide
    mouths agape and bared teeth flashing.

    It's an hour of satisfying
        runs and flying
ambitions, as gravity's
    traction relaxes a little
        and hunting tigers freeze
into a fine, deepening
tensity, muscles marshalling
    toward that signal opportune instant

        when the commanding soul emerges:
            Now—
                    Now, it urges,
    and the breaking body slides
        upon the air's broad back
            and hangs there, rides and rides
    with limbs outstretched—but claws
    bedded in their velvet-napped paws,
        for there will be no killings tonight.

        All bloodshed is forbidden
            here. . . .
                    That's the hidden
    message of these grounds, which threads
        like a stream around the pines
            and rocks and iris-beds.
    The danger's all a bluff, an
    artful dumb show staged by a clan-
        destine family of tigers

        with Chinese dragon faces,
            whose grimaces
    and slashing, cross-eyed glances serve
        to conceal the grins that beckon
            you into the preserve
    of a rare, ferociously
    playful mind. Enter. You are free
        from harm here. There's nothing to fear.

IN A JAPANESE MOSS GARDEN

    After a night of rain
      this garden so
fragile it's never raked, but swept,
      lies on a bed
soft as itself, and all the morning, fed
by the rain banked richly below,
      bathes in a glow

    gentle as candle-light.
      Variety's
ascendant in this lowland where
      a hundred-plus
plush samples of the like-velutinous—
star-shaped mosses, amulets, keys,
      bells, snowflakes—ease

    toward freshly minted greens
      which have no one-
word names: rust- or russet-green, pump-
      kin-tangerine-,
copper- and pewter-, frost- and fire-green. . . .
No land was ever overrun
      more mildly, none

    yielded with more repose:
      an intertwined,
inclusive, inch-by-inch advance
      built this retreat
where stones are put to rest beneath a sheet
of nap, where limbs are under-lined,
      and where the mind

    meets not tranquillity
      merely, but some
dim image of itself—the rounded
      mounds, the seams dense
with smaller seams, the knit, knobbed filaments
all suggesting the cranium,
      as witnessed from

within. But now this web
of imagery
bends with a newcomer the colours
of an unripe
tomato who, beast of another stripe,
untended and rootlessly free,
apparently,

runs, runs, runs without rest.
His body gleams
with those pellucid lusters found
within a night's
last vistas, when a dyeing dawn alights
upon your lids, flooding your dreams,
until it seems

your inborn sights and pigments
outshine the day;
it's morning in a Japanese
moss garden and
a creature blazing like a firebrand
now makes its episodic way
between a grey

stand of toadstools that lean
like headstones, through
a swampy heel-print, up a fallen
leaf (and then back
down when it proves an airy cul-de-sac),
across a root, a stump, a dew-
drenched avenue

of shorter moss that looks
and feels like felt . . . .
Inanimate, the garden may
better have met
the thoughtful ends on which its lines are set,
but if its motionlessness must
come to a halt,

    what cause more fitting than
     this zigzag creature,
  bizarre as anything in Nature,
      whose home's a firma-
mental network, a plane of lifelines pitched
upon a random set of reference
     points, a maze which in its

    closed-in stringiness makes
     a self-portrait?
One might view him as captive, too,
    like any prey
inside his web, yet still take heart at the way
he runs to the task, as if to say,
     Today's the very

    day for weaving finally
     a tapestry
at once proportionate and true.

A FLIGHT FROM OSAKA

Into the translucent, smudged, omnivorous wheel
    That the propeller's become
Now slides, block on block and brightly unreal,
    The highflung reaches of sun-dazed Kobe,
        On whose big bay

On this early-summer Sunday afternoon some
    Playfully downscaled freighters
Are lugging broad, ballooning wakes in from
    And out to sea.... Quite a leisurely scene
        (Or so when seen

From a few miles up), with one neat, upending touch
    Of real loveliness: the way
Those wakes suggest jet streams—only so much
    Slower to gather, to shatter, to wear
        Themselves out where

Each least impulse is translated into a dense,
    Earthbound medium. The weight,
The piled resistance of those depths, presents
    Us with another, plainer image: one
        Of a hard-won

And never finished struggle with a stone- and vine-
    Strewn soil, a primitive plough
Scratching out, foot by foot, its thin lifeline—
    Into which our buried forebears scattered seeds.
        The past recedes

Much as the circling world does from the round
    Windows of a plane, expanding
As it dwindles into the background, turning
    Both more mysterious and more finely
        Drawn, finally.

SEASIDE GREETINGS

(OKI ISLANDS, JAPAN SEA)

Together waking to the smell
of new mats beneath us, we find our clothes,
quickly dress, and in slippers shuffle
    down the dark hall

to the entryway, where we trade
slippers for shoes, slide the front
door free, and steal outside
    without a sound.

Our fishing village has not woken
much before us; day is in the splendid,
splashy process of breaking
    over an open

sea and over flooded ricefields
become lavender mirrors, snugly
secured by little green studs.
    We have big pads

of paper bundled under our arms—off
to sketch Yoroi Iwa,
Armour Rock, the crest of a bluff
    which, just as if

something with endless time to kill
on this outpost island had been
engineering an epochal
    if rather small

joke, not only looks like armour but in
its boxy, braided lines is closer
to the Japanese style than
    the European.

Of course given the scale Nature has
to work with, all of these uncanny,
and often funny, resemblances
    (the ancient trees

  wrung like buxom women, whales
in the clouds, bights like laughing
horses' heads, potatoes bearing profiles
   of generals

  dead now for centuries) are
statistical certainties, nothing
more, and yet they do appease our
   appetite for

  play at the stone heart of things—
a loose, elusive spirit not
about to shimmer its mica wings
   in our smudged drawings.

  Under a midday sun we climb
a treeless, grasshopper-ridden hill
whose summit drops headlong as doom
   to the torn rim

  of the sea a hundred yards or so
below. Hawks ride in the updrafts
and test us with unnervingly
   low, virtuoso

  swoops and passes, so near we can discern
how the jumpy eyes pivot in their heads.
Their motions have no waste—glide and turn
   as though they're borne

  upon a refined physics,
an applied mathematics streamlining
toward the pure. We watch their slow arcs
   and plunging strikes,

  cheered to see them flutter
up with empty claws; while nothing we've
ever seen goes about the search for
   a meal with more

  inspiriting grace, our sympathies
are with the homely, camouflage-
seeking mouse, rather than with these
   ferocious beauties.

... Dusk is something taking place
at unreachable distances,
moving off at one remove from us,
 who raptly focus,

 with the fixity of the deservedly
ravenous, on the feast being set
before us—rice, squash, spinach in soy
 and sesame,

 sweet ribbons of squid strewn
with pinhead-sized pink fish eggs, pickles,
a sea-bream sliced for sashimi and then
 fitted back in

 around the bones to restore
its swimming shape, a clear soup, bamboo
shoots, lotus root, and two half-litre
 bottles of beer.

 Loaned kimono-like robes hold in
the heat from our baths as we eat,
and as we retire to an embracing
 sudden exhaustion

 larger than we are. Within
each other's arms we lie, neatly, indeed
almost palindromically, placed: settling
 in in an inn . . . .

 The phrase, nearly perfect, is perfect for
tomorrow's postcards, those shiny seaviews
for our friends that might begin, 'Dear ——,
 It's lovely here.'

ON A SEASIDE MOUNTAIN

(OKI ISLANDS, JAPAN SEA)

Earlier, as if to conform
to our distant notions of what a remote
Japanese island ought to look like, a warm
sea-mist sifted in, transmuting browns and greens

into the hovering, washed-out greys
of one of those old vertical landscapes
whose ascent to the temple threads a double maze
of fog and foliage. Yet as we climb

from the coast, slips of colour filter through—
a red swatch of earth, freshly torn, a green red-
berried bush, green-gold clumps of bamboo—
and the waves' gentle papery crash drifts out

of hearing. To know that the Japanese
seven and again six hundred years ago
banished powerful emperors to these
very islands enriches the mist; far as such

kingdoms are, they'll never be nearer
than while the ground's unreally webbed with fog,
like this, and the air's a breathed-on mirror.
The hills hold, visibly, a second tale,

one—small-plotted, cyclical—of buried toil:
the scaling eye still traces terraces
where rice was grown by hand, and by the handful.
   Ahead, a fall of sunlight, washing some

of the mist from the air, unveils a crust
of prisms on a big rock outcrop. The cloud
cover's coming brightly undone at last.
It's rainbow weather. The bands are there, just

waiting for the right touch of sun.
Yet as we round another bend, the sight we're
treated to is something else again:
a horse, a chunky tan palomino

with milky mane and a calm, discerning
fix to the eyes. The creature stamps, as if
commanding us to halt, which we do, returning
its gauging stare. It expels a long, low

importunate snuffle; then, as if it wants
to make itself perfectly clear, repeats
this sound and, ears up, waits on our response.
None forthcoming, it rears its head, utters a keen

unnerving squeal that seems to hold a bit
of laughter, plunges around (admitting
a glimpse of bobbing genitals, as this *it*
becomes a *he*) and clatters off.... He doesn't

go far. A short ways up the mountainside
he stops for us—until we near. Again he's
gone; again he stops. He's become our guide,
apparently. In any case, we follow him

while the remaining mist burns into the sun
until we reach a circular outlook high
above the sea, where nine horses, including one
pony whose mane's so short it stands erect, are

grazing. Head down, duties done, our leader glides
in among his comely fellows, none of whom
show much alarm at having us at their sides.
They huddle closer perhaps, but, snouts in clover,

carry on with the business of the day.
It's so quiet we can hear their surf-like breathing.
   Below, though worn white at the rim of the bay,
the sea by sheer drops precipitately builds

toward an unsounded blue, deeper than the sky's,
richer than mist or history. Whenever
one of these horses lifts its thoughtful eyes
from the turf, stems trailing from its mouth,

this is the view. They eat slowly. The sun's pace
is perfectly theirs, and the planted ease
they are breathing, are breeding, in this place,
while not meant for us, lightens us anyway.

TWO INCIDENTS ON AND OFF GUAM

I.

Nothing was going to seem very
Strange after that extraordinary
Drive down to the beach in the back
Of a jeep, the road snaking
Through huge cross-sections of jungle even
Denser than what we'd seen before,
Uppermost fronds a dazzling, rich
White-bronze in that tropical sun, grey
Those further down, and nearly black
The warring undergrowth in which
Windfall coconuts lay
Like so many old, flaking
Helmets from that other War;

So that, when we found everyone
On the beach standing right
At the water's edge, watching the sea,
We fell in unquestioningly,
Gazes drifting until we too
Spotted in the distance, where
The sea was whitecapped, a pair
Of bobbing swimmers. They
Were drowning. A simple truth—but one
We couldn't grasp at first, nor quite
Grasp that the only thing to do
Was to stand and wait. A radio
Call had gone out . . . . Help was on the way.

Help, at last, took the splendid,
Hearteningly larger-than-life form
Of a helicopter ripping across
The sky to come to a high, suspended
Clattering halt and release a fine
Rope ladder that landed just outside
The swimmers' reach. Now commenced

That clumsy, exacting process—so
Brutally, so agonizingly slow—
Of attempts at linkage; each new toss
Of the ladder falling wide,
As the fading swimmers flailed against
The pull of their local storm,

Until somehow, as we stood there
Watching, that deep, tortuous bond between
Man the maker and his machine
Was pared to a dangling thread,
And right before our eyes a half-dead
Body like a fish was hoisted through
The glittering, naked air
To the copter's belly—leaving two
All but disembodied arms to thrash
In the sunny scatter and smash,
The stunned smash and scatter of the sea.
   Now horrifying, hypnotizing
As this was, it was, finally,

Unreal as well, as though
We were watching a film-clip, some
Snippet of the evening news . . .
The entire ordeal—the bare
Line dropped again, then again, and then
That second swimmer delivered from
His gasping burial—at once so
Stirring, and so *unreal*:
Even as we yelled, whistled, clapped
Our hands, somehow still to feel,
As in a moviehouse, that we'd been
Played on by a drama whose
Performers were never there.

II.

The rubber feet pinch,
the window of the mask is scratched. Easing
out of my element, I inch
down the aluminium ladder

on the side of the boat,
legs trailing loose in the warm sea,
let go, drop and turn and float
successfully on my stomach. I send a blast

of air up the snorkel, spouting a crown
of salty water that, after
a looping pause, comes down
sweetly on my back, and begin, flush

with the reserved, lazing
powers of my new frog's feet, to coast
upon the surface. Under this blazing
noon sun the sea's so calm it can scarcely be

the medium in which, just three days ago,
those two swimmers I keep thinking about
were nearly drowned. The water's so
tranquil today you could swim out

for miles, it seems, letting it hold
you high like a child, aloft and kicking
in a parent's upraised arms. Assorted spilled
pastels, dissolved of all

material commitments, flicker and glide
in the bay's upper reaches;
today the sea's wide-
open and the sun goes clear

to the rolling coral stone-
garden, some forty feet below, where
three divers in black wet-suits, two men
and the boyishly slighter

figure of a woman, drift to and fro,
poking about, exchanging
sweeping, emphatic messages by way
of hand-signals. As enticing

as that sea-floor looks, still
more so—a grace to place
against any anemone's—are those tall
wavering columns of bubbles

rising from the divers' air-tanks;
while risibly like the thought-balloons
one meets in comic books
and animated cartoons, they possess

a lissomeness, a vinelike
elevating loveliness that pulls me
closer. And when I flutter-kick
over to where the bubbles break

the surface, nosing my mask right
into that climbing line of hundreds
and hundreds of spirited white
beads of light,

something marvellous transpires: I am—again—
reminded of film, the colourless
televisions of my boyhood, that endless run
of laugh-tracked comedies in which

with some low-budget hocus-pocus
(the camera, to the strum of a harp,
slipping out of focus,
or a panning swing toward the centre

of a painted target- or pin-
wheel-shape that would then
begin to spin)
one was forever being promoted

to those selective sectors
where cumulus banks are firm enough
for walking, a white sheet is every actor's
home- and office-apparel alike, and one finds

each humble face laughably
unaltered—bespectacled or buck-toothed,
bald or bulbous-nosed as the case may be, but *happy*,
for this is Heaven.... And to this vision

while I floated simply
in the warm blizzard of a stranger's
exhalations, body limply
open to the sea's slight suggestive nudgings,

came another, of which the first, for all
its silliness, was a kind of clue, a parody
whose unsullied original
might be obliquely

glanced at, indeed
had been glimpsed already,
for there was a sense of having peered
before into one of these

miraculous pristine

passages that wait beside you
always, if only it were known *which*
floorboard to take the crowbar to,
which stone uproot on the hillside, if only

you dared to; *this* tunnel, here, into a breath-
taking incandescence so intense the
body is as nothing in the path
of its streaming, weightless and homeless and

helpless, hopeful and afraid.

OXFORD POETS

Fleur Adcock
Yehuda Amichai
James Berry
Edward Kamau Brathwaite
Joseph Brodsky
Basil Bunting
D. J. Enright
Roy Fisher
David Gascoyne
David Harsent
Anthony Hecht
Zbigniew Herbert
Thomas Kinsella
Brad Leithauser
Herbert Lomas
Medbh McGuckian
Derek Mahon

James Merrill
John Montague
Peter Porter
Craig Raine
Tom Rawling
Christopher Reid
Stephen Romer
Peter Scupham
Penelope Shuttle
Louis Simpson
Anne Stevenson
Anthony Thwaite
Charles Tomlinson
Andrei Voznesensky
Chris Wallace-Crabbe
Hugo Williams